W9-CHT-307

PEOPLES OF THE ANCIENT WORLD

Life in

Ancient South America

Hazel Richardson

Crabtree Publishing Company
www.crabtreebooks.com

Crabtree Publishing Company
www.crabtreebooks.com

For Eben, Oliver, and Thomas

Coordinating editor: Ellen Rodger
Project editor: Rachel Eagen
Editors: Carrie Gleason, Adrianna Morganelli
Production coordinator: Rosie Gowsell
Production assistance: Samara Parent
Scanning technician: Arlene Arch-Wilson
Photo research: Allison Napier
Art director: Rob MacGregor

Project Management
International Book Productions, Inc.
Barbara Hopkinson
Judy Phillips
J. David Ellis
Dietmar Kokemohr
Sheila Hall

Consultant: Brian S. Bauer, Ph.D Department of Anthropology, University of Illinois at Chicago

Photographs: Art Archive/Archaeological Museum Lima/ Dali Orti: p. 20 (right), p. 21 (top); Art Archive/Archaeological Museum Lima/ Mirelle Vautier: p. 23 (right), p. 24 (top); Art Archive/ Biblioteca Nacional Madrid/ Dagli Orti: p. 12 (bottom); Art Archive/ Ethnographical Museum Gottenburg/ Dagli Orti: p.23 (left); Art Archive/ Musee du Nouveau Monde La Rochelle/ Dagli Orti: p. 28; Art Archive/ Museo de Arte Colonial de Santa Catalina Cuzco/ Dagli Orti: p. 3; Art Archive/ Museo del Banco Central de Reserva Lima/ Dagli Orti: p. 7; Art Archive/ Museo del Oro Lima/ Dagli Orti: p. 3 (top); Art Archive/ Museo Pedro do Osma Lima/ Mirelle Vautier: p. 12 (top), p. 29 (bottom); Craig Duncan/ DDB: p. 16 (bottom); Eye Ubiqitous/ CORBIS: p. 18 (top); Werner Forman/ Art Resource, NY: p. 19; Werner Forman/ CORBIS/MAGMA: p. 18 (bottom), p. 21 (bottom); Albert Frogel: pp. 8-9, p. 16 (top); Philippe Gourmand: p. 8; Charles and Josette Lenars/ CORBIS: p. 22 (top); Logan Museum of Anthropology, Benoit College: p. 22 (bottom); Craig Lovell/ CORBIS/ MAGMA: p. 9; PromPeru Files: p. 10, p. 17, p. 25, p. 31 (bottom); PromPeru Files/ Mylene D'Auriol: p. 11 (bottom); PromPeru/ Jorge Sarmiento: p. 7 (bottom); Roman Soumar/ CORBIS/ MAGMA: pp. 4-5, p. 20 (bottom); Elias Wakan: (cover)

Illustrations: William Band: borders, pp. 4–5 (timeline), p. 6 (map), p. 10, p. 13, pp. 26–27, p. 30 (top).

Cover: Reproduction of a Chimu tapestry, or weaving.
Contents: Inca carpet with local flora and fauna design, created in the 1750s.
Title page: Machu Picchu was an Inca city that was built high in the Andes mountains. It was the last settlement to be abandoned when Spanish explorers arrived in South America in the 1500s.

Crabtree Publishing Company
www.crabtreebooks.com   1-800-387-7650

Cataloging-in-Publication Data
Richardson, Hazel.
  Life in ancient South America / written by Hazel Richardson.
    p. cm. -- (Peoples of the ancient world)
  Includes index.
  ISBN-13: 978-0-7787-2042-3 (rlb)
  ISBN-10: 0-7787-2042-X (rlb)
  ISBN-13: 978-0-7787-2072-0 (pbk)
  ISBN-10: 0-7787-2072-1 (pbk)
1. Incas--History--Juvenile literature. 2. Incas--Social life and customs--Juvenile literature. I. Title. II. Series.
  F3429.R46 2005
  985'.01--dc22
                                                    2005001100
                                                    LC

Published in the United States
PMB 16A
350 Fifth Ave.
Suite 3308
New York, NY
10118

Published in Canada
616 Welland Ave.
St. Catharines
Ontario, Canada
L2M 5V6

Published in the United Kingdom
73 Lime Walk
Headington
Oxford
0X3 7AD
United Kingdom

Published in Australia
386 Mt. Alexander Rd.
Ascot Vale (Melbourne)
V1C 3032

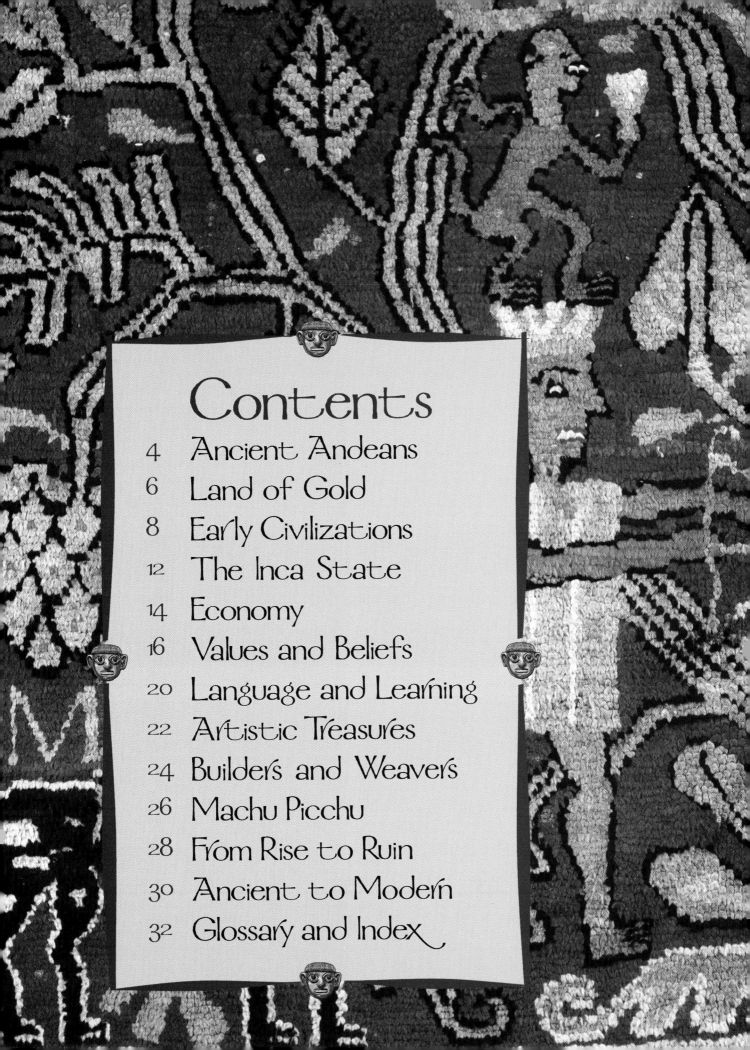

Contents

Ancient Andeans

Many ancient civilizations developed in the Andes mountains of South America. These civilizations descended from people who had migrated to the region during the last ice age. One of the most enduring Andean civilizations was the Inca empire. Over time, the Incas expanded their territory over an enormous region.

The Land Bridge

About 14,500 years ago, sea levels dropped about 330 feet (100 meters). In the Bering Strait, the waters that separate Siberia and Alaska, a land bridge linking these two areas was exposed. Groups of **nomadic** peoples crossed this bridge from Siberia and moved south through North and South America, reaching South America about 12,000 years ago.

▶ *Terrace farming was one of the ancient South Americans' most important innovations because it allowed people to grow food on steep mountainsides.*

Hunting and gathering 10,000 B.C.	Chavín 1000 B.C. - 500 B.C.	Nazca and Moche 400 B.C. - 800 A.D.	Tiahuanaco 600 A.D. - 1000 A.D.	Chimú 1100 A.D. - 1400 A.D.

▶ *The Chavín were excellent metalworkers and created many statues out of gold.*

◀ *The Moche worshipped fierce gods.*

▲ *Chimú funeral masks were placed on the faces of dead rulers when they were buried.*

Andean Civilization Arises

The first Andeans hunted animals and gathered plants for food. Over time, they settled permanently and began to farm. Around 6000 B.C., people learned how to **irrigate** fields to grow large food crops. They grew corn, squash, and chilies. The Andeans also learned to cut steps into the steep mountains, creating platforms that could be used for growing food. As populations grew, civilizations developed.

What is a "civilization?"

Most historians agree that a civilization is a group of people that shares common languages, some form of writing, advanced technology and science, and systems of government and religion.

Inca empire is founded at Cuzco and begins to expand in 1438 A.D.

▶ *Pachacuti, the ninth Inca ruler, had the city of Cuzco built.*

Spanish explorers arrive in South America in 1532 A.D.

Inca empire ends in 1572 A.D.

▶ *Spanish invaders kill Atahualpa, the Sapa Inca.*

▲ *The Spanish kill Tupac Amaru, the last Inca emperor, at Cuzco.*

Land of Gold

Many of the ancient South American civilizations developed in what is now known as the country of Peru. Seasonal floods in the river valleys made the soil rich for growing food. The Andes were plentiful with other resources that people used to improve their way of life, such as the llama and deposits of precious metals.

▲ *South America covers about 17 million square miles (44 million square km). It stretches from north of the equator to the Antarctic. The Amazon rain forest once covered almost half the continent.*

Surviving in South America

Life in the Andes was not easy. Mountain villages were shaken by earthquakes and volcanic eruptions, because the Andes range lies on a **fault line**. Life was even harder in parts of the continent where food could not be grown, such as on the dry coasts. Rain forests in the middle of the continent were difficult to clear because people did not have iron tools. The marshy mangrove swamps in the north were also unsuitable for farming because the soil was too wet.

Mountain Riches

The Andes rise up from the Pacific coast of South America. They run from Colombia to Bolivia in two chains, 120 miles (195 km) apart. High plains lie between the mountain peaks, far above sea level. The ancient Andeans grew crops on these fertile plains, or *puna*. Ancient Andeans also used stone tools to dig at mountain deposits of gold and silver. Gold nuggets, found in the Andes and in mountain streams, were melted down. The gold was then hammered into thin plates for decorating clothing, utensils, and rulers' palaces.

Harvests from the Land and Sea

The most important animal for people in the Andes was the llama, which was **domesticated** around 1000 B.C. The llama was used to carry goods along the steep mountain paths. Llama wool was spun into yarn for blankets and clothing, while llama meat, considered a delicacy, was eaten by the wealthy. Llamas were also **sacrificed** in religious ceremonies.

The first Andeans raised guinea pigs for their meat, and **alpacas** for their wool. On the coast, whales, sea lions, and fish were hunted for food. In the rain forest, people hunted animals and birds. They made colorful headdresses with feathers taken from parrots.

Terrace Farming

The steep slopes of the Andes were difficult to farm. Around 6000 B.C., the Andean people started to cut wide, flat steps into the mountains, creating terraces for planting crops. Long canals were built to channel water from mountain rivers and streams to the terraced fields. These new farming methods allowed people to grow large amounts and varieties of food, including maize, potatoes, tomatoes, peanuts, chilies, and quinoa, a cereal grain. They also grew cotton to make clothing.

◀ *This clay pot, dating from between 200 B.C. and 500 A.D., is shaped like a llama transporting goods on its back.*

▶ *Ancient Andeans wove llama wool into warm clothing. Llamas are still found in the Andes, which is the longest mountain chain in the world.*

Early Civilizations

The peoples of ancient South America built well-planned cities out of mud bricks and blocks of stone. Huge pyramids and temples were built to honor gods the people worshiped. Farmland surrounding the ancient cities was used to grow staple crops.

The Chavín Civilization

Historians believe that the Chavín, a farming people, were the first Andean civilization. The Chavín were skilled metalworkers, weavers, and potters. They used **ceramic** stirrup spout pots to hold tea and other liquids. Spout pots have a U-shaped handle and pouring spout. **Archaeologists** have found them in Chavín graves, which means that the Chavín believed they would use these pots in the **afterlife**. The Chavín also invented weaving methods, used by all later Andean societies.

◀ *The Chavín worshiped cat-faced gods, as shown on this stone carving.*

The Fierce Moche

From 400 B.C. to about 800 A.D., the Moche people lived in the coastal river valleys of northern Peru. The Moche gained control over territory by warring with other peoples. They built two temple pyramids in their capital, Galindo. One temple was built for the sun, Huaca del Sol, and one was for the moon, Huaca del Luna.

The Mysterious Nazca

The Nazca people lived along the southern coast of Peru from about 400 B.C. to 750 A.D. They built a large religious complex known as Cahuachi. They carved huge drawings on the coastal plains which fascinate archaeologists, as do the ruins of Cahuachi. The Nazca also made beautiful pottery.

The Chimú Culture

From 1100 A.D. to 1400 A.D., a civilization known as the Chimú controlled northern Peru. The Chimú were a farming people who later fought with neighboring civilizations for territory. They took many prisoners of war during these battles. The Chimú built irrigation canals and roads between their cities. The Chimú were defeated by the Incas in 1475.

The Powerful Incas

The Inca civilization arose in the Cuzco Valley of the Andes around 1000 A.D. The powerful Inca army was highly organized and was used to help **conquer** other peoples. By 1527, the Inca **empire** was the largest South America had ever known. The Incas ruled more than ten million people in an area that stretched from modern-day Ecuador to Chile. Some Inca buildings still stand in the Cuzco Valley.

The Rich Tiahuanaco

From 600 A.D. to 1000 A.D., the Tiahuanaco people lived in the Andes mountains in what are now Peru and Bolivia. Historians named these peoples after their capital city, Tiahuanaco. The city was first settled around 300 A.D., near the shores of Lake Titicaca. The Tiahuanaco were a rich and powerful civilization. They built massive pyramids and temples using giant carved stones. Parts of their temple walls were covered with gold.

▲ *The entrance to the temple at the ruins of Tiahuanaco, in modern-day Bolivia.*

▼ *The Pyramid of the Sun, at the Moche capital city, Galindo, was built with mud bricks.*

Social Structure

High priests were the most important members in ancient Andean societies. They performed religious ceremonies. People believed the high priests were closest to the gods, and that they could influence events such as rain or earthquakes by talking to the gods. Nobles and **administrators** made up a ruling class that helped keep order. Priests, architects, and army leaders worked under the nobles. Artisans produced pottery, textiles, and metal goods. Farmers and laborers made up the largest class.

Homes and Palaces

Coastal homes were built of wooden posts that were covered in mud. The roofs were flat and **thatched** with grass. Mountain homes were made of stone blocks, with peaked thatched roofs to let the rain run off. The rulers' palaces were located in city centers. They were made of stone, and parts of their outer walls were covered with gold.

High Priest

Nobles

Priests, Architects, and Army Leaders

Artisans

Farmers and Laborers

▲ *People in ancient Andean societies were organized under a strict social structure.*

◄ *Inca houses, such as this mountain home, had no furniture. People slept on llama wool or grass mats.*

Food and Drink

Ancient Andeans ate their main meal in the evening. The meal was usually a stew made of potatoes, beans, and other vegetables, such as maize, or corn, peppers, squash, and chilies. On festival days and other special occasions, people roasted maize cobs and guinea pigs. The most common drink for both children and adults was *chicha*, a mild beer made from **fermented** maize.

Making Cloth

On the coast, where it was warmer, people grew cotton and wove it into fabric to make clothing. In the mountains, cloth was woven from llama wool. Nobles wore clothing made from the fine wool of the alpaca or vicuna, animals similar to llamas. Dyes made from plants, and cochineal, a type of insect, were used to color fabric purple and red. **Iron oxide** was used to dye fabric orange. Textiles were woven with **geometric** patterns of lines, animal shapes, and plants. Gold and silver thread was stitched into the clothing worn by the ruling classes.

Styles of Dress

Men wore a wraparound skirt and a simple shirt, or a knee-length tunic, sometimes with a woolen poncho over top to keep warm. Women wore ankle-length dresses and a shawl. Both men and women wore sandals made of llama hide or slippers woven from grass. Nobles decorated themselves with gold and silver necklaces and bracelets. People of all ages and social classes wore caps called *chucus*, woven from llama or alpaca wool. These were often fastened to the head with a woven headband.

Women and Children

Inca women tended to the crops in the fields, and took care of the animals. Mothers strapped their babies onto their backs so they could work in the fields and look after their children at the same time. Children were expected to work from an early age. They helped their parents by doing tasks, such as keeping animals away from the crops and taking care of the llamas.

▲ *Maize was a staple crop in the Andes.*

▸ *Andean peoples still wear colorful woven shawls, as their ancestors did.*

The Inca State

Ancient South American civilizations were ruled by high priests or kings. Most people were farmers or artisans who supported the rulers and their families by giving them food and items they produced. Few details are known about the way the earliest South American societies were run. Historians know most about Inca government from the writings of Spanish conquistadors.

The Greatest Emperor

At first, the Incas controlled only the land around their capital, Cuzco. In 1438, Cuzco was attacked by a neighboring people, the Chanca. The Inca ruler, called the Sapa Inca, fled the city, but his son, Yupanqui, led the army to defeat the Chancas. Yupanqui changed his name to Pachacuti, meaning "he who changed the world," and ruled the Incas for 30 years.

Land of Four Parts

By 1480, millions of people lived within the Inca empire. The empire was so large that it was divided into four regions. Close male relatives of the Sapa Inca were made lords of each region. The lords made up a council that advised the Sapa Inca on important matters.

▶ *Pachacuti expanded the Inca empire into Ecuador, Bolivia, and Chile.*

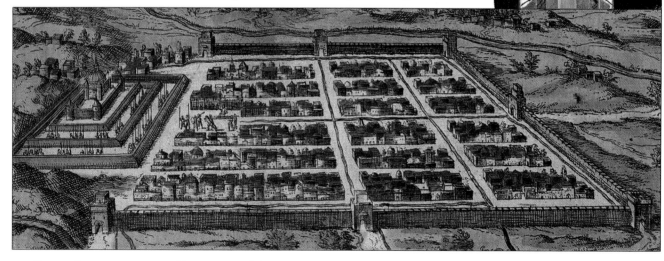

▲ *Cuzco began as a small town and became a large, magnificent city.*

Curacas, the Local Lords

The empire's four regions were divided into many **provinces**. Each province was run by a governor, who was a male member of the Sapa Inca's family. The governor appointed administrators, or *curacas*, to run the households in his province. *Curacas* were in charge of the land each household was given to farm, and made sure taxes were paid. *Curacas* supervised many households. Leaders of peoples who were conquered by the Incas were often made *curacas*. *Curacas* could be men or women.

Conquered Peoples

The Incas developed their large empire by taking over land that was lived on by other peoples. Some peoples were happy to join the Inca empire, because they knew they would be given food and housing in return for their labor. Those unwilling to join the Inca empire were conquered anyway, but they were allowed to keep some of their customs as well as their languages. Conquered peoples were taught Inca farming and weaving techniques, and paid taxes to the emperor as the Incas did.

Crime and Punishment

Theft was rare in the Inca empire, as people were given what they needed by the government. When they did occur, crimes were harshly punished. Thieves had their hands and feet cut off. Each day they were carried to the city gates and left to beg for food. Murderers were thrown to their deaths off cliffs.

Mountain Runners

Inca administrators could not communicate with each other easily because the empire was so large, and there were no vehicles or horses to travel the length of the empire. Trained runners, called *chasquis*, were used to deliver messages between government administrators. *Chasquis* were stationed in small stone huts that stood every four miles (6.5 km) or so on the Inca road network, the Royal Road. These huts, called *tambos*, had food and water supplies for the *chasquis*. When a *chasqui* received a message, he ran as fast as he could to the next *tambo* and gave the message to the *chasqui* there. Messages could be carried about 150 miles (240 km) a day like this.

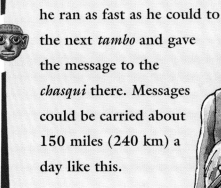

▶ Chasquis *were also used to deliver special goods, such as fresh fish, to the Sapa Inca.*

Economy

Ancient South Americans did not use money. People traded with each other for the things they needed, such as food, tools, and cloth. This is known as the barter system. The Inca work force was so well organized that they produced all that they needed and did not have to trade with peoples outside their empire.

The Allyus

The Sapa Inca controlled all of the land in the empire. Plots of land were given to groups of families called *allyus*. The families of an *allyu* worked together to farm the land. Men caught fish and other seafood on the coasts. Women either helped in the fields or wove textiles that were worn, traded, or buried with the dead. Artisans within the *allyu* made pottery vessels from clay, and gold ornaments that were worn by the ruling class.

Dividing the Land

Each Inca community was divided into three parts. Harvests from one part were distributed among the people so that everyone was fed. Crops from the other two portions of farmland were given to nobles and administrators. Llama and alpaca herds were divided among the people in the same way. Every family received all the food, housing, and wool it needed. If a crop failed, the people were given food from the government's supply.

▲ *Men from each* **allyu** *were chosen to serve in the Inca army. Early in the Inca empire, men went into the army after harvesting their crops. As the empire grew, men had to leave their* **allyus** *for several years.*

Inca Taxes

People received land, housing, wool, and food from the Inca government. As payment, people had to pay taxes to the government in the form of either labor or goods. Each year, men worked for a set number of days under a system of public service called *mita*. Some panned for gold in streams, while others built irrigation canals, roads, and temples. Artisans were required to make a certain amount of goods, such as pottery and jewelry, for their Inca rulers each year. Women wove cloth in their homes and sent the finest textiles to the ruling class as tax payment.

Trade

Llamas were used as pack animals to carry goods between communities. Llamas carried up to 70 pounds (32 kg) of goods loaded in baskets on their backs. Caravans traveled on stone roads first built by earlier civilizations. The Incas traded with the **indigenous** peoples of the Amazon rain forest, swapping bronze tools and gold for monkeys and colorful feathers.

▲ *The ancient South Americans made gold statues and jewelry. Gold lured Spanish explorers into the region in the late 1500s.*

◄ *The Incas built roads that criss-crossed the Andes so they could travel through the mountains. The road network was called the Royal Road, and eventually ran the length of the Inca empire, covering over 14,000 miles (22,500 km).*

Values and Beliefs

The ancient South Americans believed in many gods, and thought that spirits lived in rivers, mountains, and other parts of nature. These early civilizations mummified their dead, made sacrifices to honor their gods, and prayed to the gods for protection from enemies and natural disasters.

Shamans

Shamans were spiritual leaders who performed ceremonies to cure the sick, make **prophecies**, and control volcanic eruptions, floods, and other natural events. Chavín shamans made a powder from a cactus, then inhaled it through hollowed-out animal bones to put themselves into **trances**. Shamans believed that by doing this, they became jaguars and could perform magic. Moche shamans called on animal spirits to help solve problems, such as defeating enemies and coping with drought, or periods of little rain. They also wore jaguar masks and chanted to the gods for help. Inca shamans drank a tea brewed from bark and plants that made them dream and make prophecies.

▲ El Brujo was one of the gods of the Moche. The Moche honored him by sacrificing prisoners of war.

Ancient Andean Gods

As early as 2000 B.C., the Andean peoples worshiped a god known as the staff god. Later, both the Chavín and Nazca worshiped this god. He had fangs and claws, and held a staff, or stick. Some historians believe that the Incas adapted the staff god into Viracocha, their god of creation, since images of Viracocha look like the staff god. The Incas believed that Inti, their sun god, was the giver of life, and that the Sapa Inca was **descended** from him.

◀ Shamans wore jaguar masks when performing religious rituals.

The Nazca Lines

The Nazca created huge designs on the coastal plains of Peru. They cleared the red surface soil to reveal lighter soil underneath, creating line patterns and images of humans, spiders, monkeys, and birds. They also drew straight lines thousands of feet long. Some of these lines spread outward from a single spot like spokes on a wheel. These patterns are known as ray centers. Some historians believe that the Nazca lines were prayers to the gods for rain.

Sacrifices

The ancient Andeans killed humans and animals as sacrifices and offered the bodies to their gods. They believed this would please the gods and prevent earthquakes and other disasters, and also ensure good crops. The Moche sacrificed prisoners of war, removed the flesh from the bodies, and hung the skeletons in their temples. The Incas sacrificed children by burying them alive on mountaintops, where it was believed they would become mountain gods.

The Nazca lines are so big that their designs can only be seen from the air. The patterns have survived thousands of years because the dry plains of Peru receive such little rain.

▶ Inca cities had a stone pillar, or **intihuatana,** *which means "for tying the sun." Some historians believed that the pillars were used in ceremonies on the winter solstice, to keep the sun "tied" closer to the Earth. Many historians do not share this belief today.*

Mummies

The ancient Andeans mummified their dead rulers and nobles. They believed that their rulers were gods who could protect them, even in death. Coastal civilizations, including the Nazca and the Moche, made mummies by drying bodies in the arid desert air. The mountain civilizations, including the Incas, freeze-dried the bodies of their nobles in the cold mountain air. The cold air mummified the bodies, which are called ice mummies. Most of the mummies were buried in a sitting position, wrapped in blankets.

▼ *The Moche made pottery masks in the shape of jaguar heads, similar to this illustration.*

The Afterlife

Ancient burial sites show that the early Andeans believed people continued to live in another world, called the afterlife, after they died. Peasants were wrapped in simple cotton cloth and buried with the tools they would need for working in the afterlife. Graves of rulers were filled with gold and silver utensils, jewelry, pottery jars, and beautiful woven cloth.

▶ *Moche rulers were often buried with hundreds of decorated clay pots.*

▲ *The Incas believed that the bodies of the dead were sacred. The dead were buried in a sitting position, and their faces were sometimes covered with masks.*

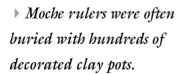

The Sapa Inca

The ruler, or **emperor** of the Incas, was called the Sapa Inca. He performed religious ceremonies on special occasions, such as the first plowing of the fields in spring. The Sapa Inca was believed to be descended from the sun god, Inti, and was worshipped by his people as a god. Traditionally, the Sapa Inca married his eldest sister, who became known as the Coya. The Sapa Inca also had many other wives. If the Sapa Inca had a son with the Coya, the child became **heir** to the throne. If the Sapa Inca did not have a son with the Coya, he chose one of his other sons to be the next emperor.

Life of the Sapa Inca

Each Sapa Inca had a palace built for him in the capital city, Cuzco. When a Sapa Inca traveled, servants carried him on a golden **litter** lined with colorful feathers. Women and children walked ahead of him, sweeping the ground, playing music, and strewing flowers. His face was hidden by fabric because his appearance was thought to be too powerful for humans to see. When a Sapa Inca died, his body was mummified and kept in his palace. During religious festivals, the body was paraded through the streets of Cuzco.

Becoming an Adult

Children of Andean societies became adults and could marry as soon as they reached **puberty**. Inca boys from noble families had to take lessons on Inca tradition and **morals**. They were tested to prove their intelligence and courage. If they passed the test, they were given a weapon, such as a spear, and earplugs to show that they had become men.

The Incas' Long Ears

Earplugs were pieces of metal, such as gold, or pieces of shell, that men pushed through their earlobes like earrings. This made their earlobes longer. Moche and Inca men wore earplugs to show their status in society. When Spanish explorers came to Peru, the custom was still practiced. The Spanish called Inca noblemen "long ears" because of this custom.

▲ Inca noblemen and curacas wore earplugs to show their social status.

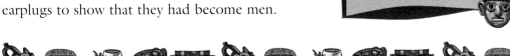

Language and Learning

Hundreds of cultures lived in and around the Andes mountains, many with their own language. Ancient South American societies did not have writing systems so they used storytelling and other methods to record information. Important facts, such as taxes, were recorded on a string called a *quipu* using a system of knots.

Quipus

The Incas recorded information by using a *quipu*, a long string with shorter, colored strings tied to it. Each color represented something, such as corn, and the different types of knots represented numbers. Administrators in each Inca province used the *quipu* system to record the number of births and deaths in the province, as well as the amount of woven cloth sent to Cuzco as tax. *Quipu* was also used to keep track of the size of llama herds and the amount of grain that farmers grew. The *quipus* were carried to Cuzco by *chasquis*. Although historians know what kind of information was recorded on *quipus*, they do not know how to **decode** them.

▶ *Ancient South Americans, such as the Chimú, often depicted details about the way their gods looked and what they did on textiles.*

◀ *Women wove colorful wool or cotton belts by hand using a backstrap loom, which was a loom tied to their waists with a belt.*

Learning

Children in ancient South America learned practical skills by helping adults with their work. Children helped plant and harvest crops in the fields, and they also helped women with household tasks, such as preparing meals. They learned about their culture by listening to stories and legends told by the **elders**. The Incas sent only children of nobles to school. Sons of noble Inca families went to school in Cuzco for four years to learn the Quechua language. They also took lessons in history, religion, astronomy, and mathematics. Daughters of noble families were sometimes chosen to work in the temples, where they were taught to weave textiles and make objects from gold, such as ceremonial masks.

Inca Languages

The Incas allowed conquered peoples to speak their own languages, but they also insisted that everyone learn and understand the Inca language, Quechua. This was the language used by the Inca government. Among themselves, people spoke their native language. There were over 700 languages spoken within the Inca empire. One of these, Aymara, is the official language of modern-day Bolivia. Quechua is still spoken by millions of people in South America today.

▲ *A* **quipucayamoc** *was an expert in making and decoding* **quipus.** *It took four years of study to become a* **quipucayamoc.**

▶ *The* **quipu** *was a complicated method of record-keeping. Each string represented a piece of information, such as how many babies were born that year.*

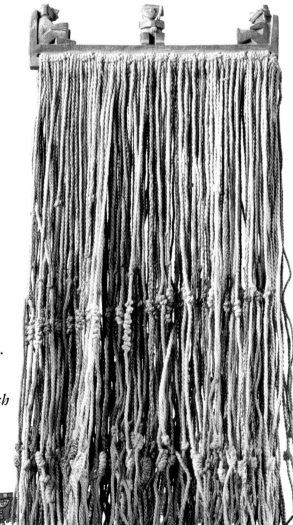

Artistic Treasures

The ancient Andeans did not have a system of writing, so historians study artwork and other artifacts to learn what life was like in ancient South America. Pottery, textiles, and metalwork showed scenes from everyday life, such as hunting, battles, worship, and the lives of rulers.

Chavín Crafts

The Chavín decorated their pottery with a variety of carefully repeated patterns, including figure eights, circles, and curls. Simple figures of people and animals were also common. The Chavín were expert goldsmiths. They hammered gold into thin sheets, which they shaped into masks and pots. They also wove alpaca wool into beautiful rugs and blankets. Alpaca textiles were valuable and were mostly owned by priests and nobles. The Chavín decorated their textiles with the same patterns as their pottery. They also made a musical instrument by punching small holes into a large seashell. A musician played the instrument by blowing into the shell, like a trumpet, and covering the holes with his or her fingers to create different notes.

▲ Moche portrait vessels were shaped using a mold, but the facial features were crafted by hand, and no two were alike. The faces often had tattoos on them.

▶ The Chavín used the stirrup spout pot to store and serve liquids, such as **chicha.**

Moche Pottery

The Moche are known for their lifelike three-dimensional portrait vessels, crafted to depict priests and rulers. These vessels, which were placed in the graves of dead rulers, were usually of heads only, but sometimes showed the full body. The Moche also made spout pots, like the Chavín, decorating them with vivid scenes of battles, religious ceremonies, and everyday life. Images of warriors show that the Moche used clubs and shields as weapons.

Inca Metalwork

The Incas were the most advanced metalworkers of all the ancient Andean civilizations. Artisans used bronze and copper to make spearheads and tools, such as knives. They made ceremonial masks, dishes and pots, jewelry, and even thread from gold and silver. These precious metals were so plentiful that the Incas covered parts of their palaces and temples with gold. Life-size gold and silver statues of llamas, corn stalks, and female figures stood in the courtyards of the most important temples.

Nazca Textiles

The Nazca peoples were expert weavers of cotton and llama and alpaca wool. They created fine lace and enormous pieces of textile. The cloth was woven with brightly colored geometric figures of birds, animals, and people. Textiles were used to make head coverings that protected the head and neck from the sun. They were also used as robes for wrapping the dead.

▲ This llama figurine was made out of thin sheets of gold. Llamas were a common image in Inca art. They were often made with a simple body but a detailed face. Statues were usually hollow.

◁ The Nazca decorated their textiles with images of their gods.

Builders and Weavers

The ancient Andeans were expert architects and designers. They built enormous pyramids on steep mountainsides, and irrigation canals that allowed them to grow crops in areas with almost no rainfall.

Pyramids

The ancient Andeans built enormous temples and flat-topped pyramids in their cities. The coastal civilizations, such as the Moche and the Nazca, used bricks made from mud to construct their buildings. In the mountains, people built pyramids from blocks of stone weighing up to two tons (1.8 tonnes) each. One of the most amazing structures of the Andes is the Akapana pyramid, built by the Tiahuanaco people. The stones were cut using stone and bronze tools. Great care was taken to cut the stones so they fit together perfectly, like an enormous jigsaw puzzle.

Inca Stonework

A few Inca cities, such as Machu Picchu, were not damaged at all by later European invaders. Machu Picchu consists of over 200 buildings made from granite stones that were cut to fit together. Inca cities fascinate archaeologists because the stones used to build them weigh many tons each. Such stones were found outside the Inca city of Cuzco, two miles (three kilometers) from the nearest **quarry**. Archaeologists do not know how the Incas transported these giant blocks without wheeled vehicles or horses.

▲ *Ancient Andean shamans made medicine from herbs to heal the sick.*

▸ *Machu Picchu is an Inca city that rests between two mountain peaks, 7,710 feet (2,350 meters) above sea level.*

Colorful Weaving

Ancient Andeans wove cloth from cotton and wool. The weaving looms
were easy to use, but weaving itself was complicated and time-consuming,
because the ancient Andeans wove along the vertical threads, rather than
along the horizontal threads. They chose this method because it allowed the
pattern to be clearly visible on both sides of the fabric. The threads for
weaving had to be very strong, so the yarn was spun many times. It took up to
200 hours to spin the wool for a poncho, and another 300 hours to weave the
poncho. Most women wove only one large piece of fabric each year. Textiles
were very valuable because they took so much time to make.

*▲ The Inca temple at
Pisac, near Machu
Picchu, was carefully
built from large
granite rocks. The
remains have stood for
hundreds of years.*

Inca Medicine

Inca shamans used many native plants for medicine. They used quinine, a
medicine from the bark of the cinchona tree to treat various ailments such as
fever, and roots from the ipecacuanha tree to treat poisoning. Belladonna, a
drug made from the deadly nightshade plant, was used to treat stomach
problems. These herbs were prepared as teas or **poultices**. The Incas chewed
coca leaves to dull pain and reduce fatigue.

Machu Picchu

Machu Picchu is a city high in the Andes mountains. It was built under the Inca ruler, Pachacuti, around 1460. Some historians believe that the city had religious functions, while others believe that it was built to be Pachacuti's royal summer estate. About 750 people lived there, and most were servants or artisans who worked for the Sapa Inca and the nobles who lived there. Machu Picchu was abandoned when the Spanish arrived in the mid 1500s. Machu Picchu was not found again until 1911.

1. The *intihuatana*, a carved stone that may have been used for a sun ceremony, sits on top of a rock at Machu Picchu's highest level.

2. Prayers, sacrifices, and ceremonies honoring the sun were held in the large plaza.

3. The royal compound, housing the Sapa Inca and nobles, was set apart from the other houses.

4. Most buildings and walls in the city were made of granite blocks cut using stone tools, then smoothed with sand. The blocks fit together perfectly without **mortar**.

5. Maize and other crops were grown on the terraces built on the steep mountainside. Stone irrigation canals brought water to the crops.

6. Machu Picchu sits on a ridge between two mountain peaks and is invisible from below. The ridge is located 7,710 feet (2,350 meters) above sea level.

From Rise to Ruin

The Incas established a mighty empire that brought over ten million people under one rule. The empire did not last. In 1531, hundreds of gold-seeking Spanish landed in the north of the empire. The conquistadors, who had already wiped out the native civilizations of Mexico, soon also destroyed the Inca civilization.

A Weakened Empire

The Inca emperor Huayna Capac, died around 1525. After he died, two of his sons, Huascar and Atahualpa, fought each other for the throne in a civil war that lasted five years. This war weakened the empire. In 1531, just as Atahualpa won, a Spanish conquistador named Francisco Pizarro landed with 180 men in what is now Ecuador. Pizarro was searching for the land of gold and other riches he had heard about.

The Raging Epidemic

As Pizarro and his men headed south through the empire, rumors spread. The Incas had never seen horses or guns before. They believed the Spanish had magical powers because they held "thunder and lightning" in their hands. As well as horses and guns, the Spanish brought smallpox, a disease that caused a high fever and blisters. Europeans had been exposed to smallpox for hundreds of years and so had developed some **immunity** to it. The disease was deadly to the Incas and other native peoples, who had never encountered it. The smallpox **epidemic** spread quickly, killing millions.

▲ *The Incas, especially after being weakened by smallpox, were no match for the Spanish, who had guns, strong armor, and were excellent swordsmen.*

28

▲ *Francisco Pizarro was a ruthless conquistador who conquered the native peoples of South America.*

A Spanish Trick

In 1532, Atahualpa was on his way to Cuzco to be crowned emperor when Pizarro's army captured him and his family, claiming Cuzco for Spain. The Spanish demanded a ransom for the emperor. Inca officials gave the Spanish a huge amount of gold and silver worth well over 70 million dollars today. The Spanish did not release Atahualpa as they promised. Instead, they kept him prisoner for eight months, then killed him.

End of the Empire

Manco Inca was named Sapa Inca after his half brother Atahualpa was killed. He co-operated with the Spanish at first but grew furious as they killed thousands of Incas, looted treasures, and destroyed temples. Manco Inca fled Cuzco and organized a large army of men. In 1536, he tried to retake Cuzco from the Spanish. His army, with its quilted cotton armor and spears, was no match for the Spaniards' metal armor, guns, and horses. The siege lasted months but left the Spanish victorious. Manco Inca retreated to Vilcabamba, a region northwest of Cuzco. In 1572, the Spanish killed the last Inca leader, Tupac Amaru. His death brought Inca civilization to an end.

▶ *Manco Inca formed and ruled an independent Inca state in Vilcabamba for 36 years, until he was killed by Spanish settlers.*

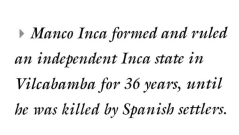

Ancient to Modern

The ancient Andeans developed ways of living that were different from other civilizations. Many of their innovations are still a part of life in South America today.

Surviving Customs

Today, millions of indigenous people live in the Andean highlands. They farm on terraces growing corn, potatoes, and peppers as their ancestors did. Many drink *chicha* and roast guinea pigs for special occasions. Peasant women weave cloth from llama wool, using the same designs as the ancient South Americans. Hand looms are still used to weave textiles.

Ancient Foods

More than half of the types of fruits and vegetables we eat were cultivated by ancient Andean farmers. Potatoes, grown on terraces in the Andes thousands of years ago, were brought back to Europe by Spanish explorers in 1565. The potato is now one of the most popular crops in the world. Other foods that originally came from ancient South America are sweet potatoes, corn, squash, many types of beans, pineapple, tomatoes, peppers, strawberries, and peanuts.

▲ *The ancient method of preserving potatoes by freezing and drying them outside is still used in the Andes today.*

▶ *Many of the vegetables, fruits, and other crops found around the world today originated in South America.*

An Ancient Ceremony

Peruvians continue to hold many traditional ceremonies, such as Qoyllur Riti. Pilgrims climb for five hours to a mountain shrine, as their ancestors did long ago. A shrine at the summit was once dedicated to the *apus*, or gods, of the mountains and hills. Today, the shrine has become an important symbol for Christians, people who follow the teachings of Jesus Christ. This shows how the Spanish, who were Christian, influenced ancient Andean beliefs.

What Mummies Tell Us

The ancient South Americans mummified their rulers in the cold, dry mountain air. The mummies have been discovered in ancient temples, wrapped in fine textiles. By examining the mummies, archaeologists have discovered many things about the life of ancient South Americans, including their diet, their clothing, and the diseases they suffered from. The bodies of sacrificed Inca children were so well preserved in the freezing mountain air that scientists have even been able to identify the last meals the children ate.

▲ *The Inca mummified their rulers and nobles, adorning them with gold headdresses and jewelry as a sign of respect and honor.*

▲ *Peruvians trek five hours to the top of a glacier during Qoyllur Riti, bringing back huge pieces of ice to be used as holy water.*

Glossary

administrator A person in charge

afterlife A life believed in many religions to continue after death

alpaca A mammal related to the llama

archaeologist A person who studies the past by looking at buildings, bones, and artifacts

ceramic A type of glazed pottery

conquer To take over by force

conquistador A Spanish conqueror

decode To translate something into a language

descend Relating to a certain family or group

domesticate To train an animal to live with humans

elder An older person or person of high status

emperor A ruler of a country or group of countries

empire A political unit that occupies a large region of land and is governed by one ruler

epidemic An outbreak of disease that spreads quickly

fault line A line of weakness in the Earth's crust

ferment To make alcohol out of food

geometric Simple designs based on squares, triangles, and circles

heir A person who receives money, property, or authority after someone's death

immunity To have protection from a disease

indigenous Native to an area

iron oxide Iron that is combined with oxygen

irrigation To supply land with water using ditches, channels, and canals

litter A large seat carried by four people

migrate To move from one region into another

morals Rules about what is right and wrong

mortar A building material used to bind stone together

nomadic Moving from place to place

poultice A thick healing paste that is placed on a cut or swollen part of the body

prophecy A message that tells the wishes of a god or predicts the future

province An administrative unit

puberty The age at which a girl becomes a woman and a boy becomes a man

quarry A place where stone is dug out of the Earth

sacrifice The act of killing an animal or person as an offering to a god in a religious ceremony

solstice A day on which the sun is farthest from the Earth's equator

staple A food that is part of a daily diet

thatched Straw or grass woven to make a roof

trance A dreamlike state of mind

Index